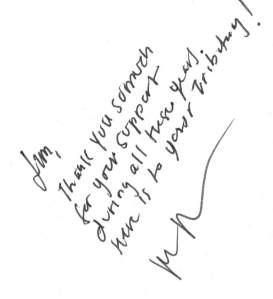

Jim,

Thank you so much
for your support
during all these years,
here is to your tributary!

TRIBUTARY

Kevin McLellan

TRIBUTARY

Kevin McLellan

Barrow Street Press
New York City

Designed by Robert Drummond
Cover photo by Tucker Hollingsworth,
   Glossy Forest Impression, Pixelation Study no. 9, Refresh
Author photo by Jonathan Sachs

Published 2015 by Barrow Street, Inc., a not-for-profit
(501) (c) 3) corporation. All contributions are tax deductible.
Distributed by:
   Barrow Street Books
   P.O. Box 1558
   Kingston, RI 02881

Barrow Street Books are also distributed by Small Press Distribution,
SPD, 1341 Seventh Street Berkeley, CA 94710-1409, spd@spdbooks.org;
(510) 524-1668, (800) 869-7553 (Toll-free within the US); amazon.com;
Ingram Periodicals Inc., 1240 Heil Quaker Blvd, PO Box 7000,
La Vergne TN 37086-700 (615) 213-3574; and Armadillo & Co.,
7310 S. La Cienega Blvd, Inglewood, CA 90302, (310) 693-6061.

Special thanks to the University of Rhode Island English Department
and especially the PhD Program in English, 60 Upper College Road,
Swan 114, Kingston, RI 02881, (401) 874-5931, which provides
valuable in-kind support, including graduate and undergraduate interns.

First Edition

Library of Congress Control Number: 2015935096

ISBN 978-0-9893296-5-1

CONTENTS

III

IV

The English language is the sea which receives tributaries from every region under heaven.

~Ralph Waldo Emerson~

It was not that long ago

That I reached me. From where
I speak now, not exactly
whole. But the mountains were

always there. The birds too. Also
once mine, flightiness. And the name-
less me. No, a wind

that has yet to appear. And a scent.
For you, I can't find
exact words. Mountains. That I go

on like this. Also, birds. Sometimes
I don't mind. That I believe. Tomorrow.
A without from where you speak.

Skin

v. **1.** And deer hides kept them warm as did a fire. With blood on their breath they fucked as a he-wolf scavenged in the background for scraps. *n.* **1.** Beside a post a cow grazes tall grass. Increasing breeze splays a fur clump caught on the outside of the barbwire fence. The clouds flash. *tr. v.* **1.** The glare. Moonlight on snow crust. The canvas. From the coop a thick-coated fox drags a now squawking and bleeding hen toward the forest's edge.

Split Personality

i.   Bouquet

The tulip wanted to be the rose
and the rose wanted to be the tulip

until both realized that as each other
they would still be cut and then

they both wanted to be a raven
on the highest branch until they

realized that they would not
bring beauty to tables.

ii.   Jugular

The foreign shapes inside

my blood: on the dizzying
track a circle becomes

light-headed: loses track of

time. My neck is in front
of who I am becoming or

rather what I have become:
circulation dictates

the how: how to not strain.

iii.   Utensils

My veins are now outside. The flying
white-necked raven with beak and talons. The feeling
to skin after a warm shower on a warm day and
breeze through an open window blows. Yet
regret doesn't exist here. Nor

does ice cream or spoons or the hands of others.

The Weight of Second Person

Language is always about loss
or absence: you only need words
when the object you want is gone.
– Jacques Lacan

As if from nowhere, many species
of birds appeared and appeared

clean. I hope to inherit this possibility.

*

A pantheon of anger: a bee

separated by a pane of glass
separated from the folds.

*

You took what I said — *hold me*
please, give us back our instant
— and placed it in your pocket

for a keepsake. Where is my dispute?

*

Three successive mornings — the
everyday of: step, stepping, stepped

— try not to look at themselves.

*

The plasticity of sleep incubates
as if for some purpose. A no-no head

shake takes the fifth. I am sorry for us.

*

Ever since the stopover, place
remained hidden and therefore you

must know these details: I did give
a "thank you" for the potted orchid

and the dank-husk smell of today
insists that I no longer recognize

the bedrock of my child-name.

Itinerary
(a tribute)

i.   the Capture

happens after desire

goes full tilt full
        circle goes past

desperation after

        a stranger comes
and offers

bull's-eyes and arrows
        and imperfection

ii.   the Encounter

        a hunter and the hunted one
picnic on fruit salad

on both borders of

        say Niagara Falls
        and "*We*"
        and
        for worse territories

ripen alongside better ones

iii.   the Sequel

a mouth

a half-moon
        where an astronaut
        refuses to land

a tongue
        where one hundred thousand craters
        hold an inarticulate

an age-old secret
        lurks and whirs
        but meanwhile an outside force
        say a breeze
        intensifies slightly
        intermittently

Silver Lake

The crime: thoughts
attaching themselves to

what is scattered in the
night sky: ground

control lost contact and
proximity: I eat sand

in hope of understanding
time: wait for rain

to pincushion the lake:
to soak the skin.

Astral Beach
(a tribute)

i.   Navel

Before I got through to me
beauty had past. (Beauty

is a finger and the desire
to be inside.) In

a stretched-to-kiss position
a stilled neck

like an astronomer
who's lost interest in sand.

This bodiless statue now
faces the night sky.

ii.   Yet the Sea Continues

The language of bodies
my body has unlearned.

Caught in its own
mollusk net

and hung out to dry.

Invisible to the hunter
who could also be me.

Almost a pearl.

iii.   Hallelujah, Hallelujah

Eyes hunt the language (echo
of the last words are roses

in an urn: in an urn

roses are no longer) the body
has forgotten. Daylight

and my neck retracts
from a series
of strangled shapes.

It had rained. Had been night.

II

Pronouns

n. 1. He is I and I is you and you is he.
2. They is us and us is we and we is they.

Watching me without you

Wind thrust-snaps

color: violence
against

the bluish-purple

door: old wound
but you

don't feel burgled:

to lie in the bed
and hear

your unmade blood:

and then another
gust:

Prologue

They beat wet clothes
against rocks
as they stand naked

is repeated for one lifetime

*

A wave that is not water
yet the wind is wind
and its whistling impairs

the ears of birds

*

The long-standing
folklore of loving
birdsong is what helps

them through night

*

Che sta andando tutto bene
(A son reached for a mother
who is not there)

Che sta andando tutto bene
(A son reaches
for a mother and she's there)

Che sta andando tutto bene
(That a son will reach
and she'll not be there)

That it is going to be okay

*

The whistling
The wet clothes
The music of again

And knowing that
not knowing (a tree grows
out of a featherbed)

follows

Fertile Earth

Still gladioli against
months of clouds. Between
rows of August a child
lies down.

The flying sticks will arrive
as scary as Oz
monkeys. To instantly
run away.

Between & against: origins
of escape & to escape
is one form
of losing one's way.

September.
Hurried is the color of plum-skin.
October.
Impatient is the color of plum-bloom.

November.

A Bedrock

Startled by not recognizing

the veins in his hands.
He didn't recognize his face

in the outside window of the

bridal shop. He won't marry
nor father. Sacrifice is a river

of perennials: tiger lilies

surrounding a stone house.
A house of stones he learned

instead of the *paso doble.*

He won't recognize himself
in another. Once he was a son.

Of Bones

I question that which
has always within been
within

versus what is also
within? when restraint
receives a signal —
the signal — to fully
surrender

the sound — the bird
against the 50 m.p.h.
windshield

— of bones

breaking — breaking

(You stopped placing me

atop your shoulders.)
(How can I trust

what I know?) (The residue

of you yelling something
hateful & then the rev
of engine & squeal of
tires & leaving in your
fuck-you pickup
truck) (I'm the son

of a gun.) (Remember when
you accused me of stealing
change from the register
where you worked. That
time you forced me to apologize
to the owners & return
this change. When in fact

while you worked I
fished for dimes and pennies
the customers dropped
and rolled under the deli-

fridge beside the register.)
(How could you not believe
me?) (Father I needed you

to believe

to believe me.)

Absence suggests being there

1.
Sedentary I remains with beloved books.
There is more than one book. Therefore

the "I" is unfaithful.

2.
No set & a child alone on a stage. *Mom?*
I am thirsty. Where is give?

[Fade to black]

3.
Stammering eye-sparkles & no words to accompany
them. These silhouettes in the long & narrow
tunnel. Yes a memory-museum. These hieroglyphs

less distinct. Less accessible.

4.
Love-me-Love-me-Love-me, a Beatles 45 skips.

5.
Sugarcane stalks. Flies whiff-inventory
their time efficiently. Yes

I am jealous.

6.
I live on top of a pillar. This vertical world

of does not or does
precipitate. That off in the distance that train with 100's of passengers chugs up

& over Salt Hill. Coal fumes rise to an already dark sky.

[Fade to white]

Plastic Speech

Your son heard your fluffy pink slippers hiss cold
    linoleum

and as you neared he pretended to sleep: a closeness
    kept

for himself. The nervous language you spoke made
    him uneasy.

For years he waits for this to change. For years he
    remains

distant. One late morning he finds a long strand of
    your hair

caught in his sweater.

To Forest Hills Station

On the platform & to

his farthest left his
birth year

1966 stands. 6:00

p.m. & now on the train
he's ⅔'s realized

from home. Yes

the end of the line is to his farthest
right & right

now — now

at this station
September can end.

Circus of one

or alone I parade —

a corkscrewing
unicyclist in cahoots

with the road —

and my vocabulary
becoming solid

when the dotted line

to the brave —
an alliance between fool

and intelligence —

repeats itself
and I know that

only humor can penetrate

the depths of a past
for the move back into me

but it's not funny

The Because

The crook of my neck: the hairline
once made a perfect cursive M:

you wept over the dishwater
in the same sink

you had once washed my infant body
(the soft machinery):

you the mother within my mother
who will not know

what I won't want you to know
is why I am:

Hydrology

i.   the Hot Facecloth

layers of dead skin
in the temporary

sudsy water rope centrifuge

my face as I knew it
went down the drain

hydrology is reliant on again

and now a new reflection
on the bottom

of the water glass

ii.   the Last Five Seconds
         (of *Die Kunst der Fuge)*

salt-and-pepper whiskers
I wait to hear (a cardinal flies
into the bathroom window
and for him the horizon goes
cockeyed) land on porcelain

iii.   Aria

the end (the end of
my face) is in my face —
brushing my clean teeth

More

the lemon

water
in your pucker

leaves you

wanting
/ you know

more / it

isn't an apt
substitute

/ it delays /

may even
hide

an actual

need in the
marrow-

drawer / yes

you are
looking into

the mirror /

with an empty
glass

in your hand

III

From Reticent's Gazebo

Red, a subjective substance in an objective shell ...
–Wassily Kandinsky

i.

A cat — under the brush — listens
to a cardinal — against a lush
landscape — slurring a sobering scat.

I do not want to be red.

ii.

A string of drool elongates
from the bull's muzzle as his
front right hoof repeatedly stamps

the ground. Nearsighted —
and from the other side
of the fence — does he see

my eyes like photographed ones
glowing red? Or does he see these veins
threading my now-skittish eyes?

iii.

Photo: in a chichi hush-hush
gay-friendly hotel my lover poses for me
on New Year's Eve in Lyon. The flash

reddens out his eyes as he stops making
our post-lovemaking and temporary bed
the first day of …

I can't remember the year. I can't remember

his friend's name — the one
who took a close-up of us — either. Fired-up
clouds inhibit the flash: blacken out our faces

except for my right eye glowing red.

iv.

The bogeyman's more frightening
to a child whose parents say, "You cannot
because you might get hurt"

and the phrases *debilitating recklessness*
and *reckless debilitation*
will be a reality for this child

as a grown-up who'll attract danger
and recognize it as romance
like a kerosene lamp in a hay barn.

v.

A pansy seed left the gazebo
for lawn
and it accepts rain.

No, not accepts. Accept implies consent ...

A red flower — a pansy
among blades
of grass — is trampled by the man.

Denouement

Under this etiolating sky &
within this 4-walled
hibernaculum he yearned

for God. Like a bronze vase
over time his patinaed
self feared resistentialism

so he untied the catgut
which kept him tied to
his unvisited bed. After

the forever of 7 long nights
the aging Sourdough
Boule & the Beaujolais

remained untouched
so he consumed
it as he was famished

for something. Something
calling & calling
his name. From within.

Seroconversion

Night sweats

and this for days
on end: how much
longer this rising

taste of bile:

a happening in
the outline of
one brief night

Copies per milliliter of blood plasma

Time broke: for now
the rain

has ceased: he forgot
to take off

the hard hat he put on
ages ago

and the arc of his neck
will verify

this: into the gutter
the helmet

grip-spins the sidewalk:
its edge:

like a young tree limb
a morning glory

creeper has in its grip
he's too close

to the history and there's
no choice but to stay:

Remarks on Nomenclature
(a tribute)

That their beauty would save me:

I never had the chance to share this
thought with any of them. As if
they knew of this responsibility

and fled tomahawk-like.

*

100's of birds (species unknown) land

on this leafless tree (species also unknown)
outside my (Homo sapiens) window.
They are ravenous this Veterans Day:

to save oneself alongside others.

*

That your pheromones …

I never had the chance to share this
thought with him because I don't know
which him emits said aroma?

As if he didn't know his own smell …

*

After those who've fled. To settle

for what one can get. Beyond to be
saved is to risk. Random flesh
inside random flesh:

to save oneself alongside others.

Breathing Room

3rd story, sound of   the opening

a sliding screen door;   sound of

flap of rooftop
pigeons' wings
reverberating   off frozen ground.

     My breath.

*

Whenyouphoneyoutalkatme.

*

Tight jeans, sunglasses,   a smirk

and his   —the once seated
French   man—
     standing
bulge to the right;
he disembarks   at St. Mary's.

     My breath.

Faux Republique

his blood
is irritable

or rather these
contaminated words:

will not speak:
his mouth

a rictus of pain:
lineaments

surface
as if for ablution

in the wake
of this morning:

he built
a cardboard village:

Morning, Morning

All the closed doors. Men

do not enter. Where is
the doorknob? Waist-high.

All men have been
distant. This. Where is

your body? Shapeless

distances near. Shapeless
distances are next to

your heart. All mornings

confirm this. All birds
outside your window.

Neither sleeping nor waking

Late afternoon
and these

necessary deafening birds

———————————

Opaque white
curtains now open

light I am envious

———————————

Floating dust particles
and the early

moon across a face

———————————

Now foreign
to me

a body always happening

18 instances of overlooking descriptors

another barn
another's

another's
northeast cage

seafaring
memories of his
all-consuming

horny
several

sick then
cold then
blank

dried
and locked yellow
city
sounding
beautiful

never a wedding

Anthology

Though this body's
stately: water

can barely recognize
me: *of course*

it's raining: this long
rain and

the moon can't be
seen: my always

salt-aching and
the surrounding

terrain: that some
don't own

their bodies: a here
where meaning

belongs to longing
and the gone:

Tributary

The fire. It is a matter
of time. I belong

to the knives. And I

must have already.
My body will need

to surrender. Like spills

around the conifers.
When a lasting visitor

mirrors slowness

and up until now
darts across my red sky.

Untitled

In a world of
unidentifiables,
as eventual, as

fleeting word, I

among the salt
& sand
& fire ants, lay

down markers
all the way to

my particular the.

IV

Parse

In a constant state of impending
you believe you're prophetic

but everyone dies:

you thwart by lionizing Halcyon
when you've only read about
the gamut of personal detritus
known by a certain few as parallax:

if you're able to recognize
from the outside in

you can either visit or pan for gold:

How to Survive a Plague

groundwater gushes the sidewalk / funnels
into the avenue / no / in reverse from here
blood follows the puckered sidewalk / licks up
contaminants / enters a recumbent body

*

chamber music + *Verde Luz* + emphatic
Ravel at St. John's = to ponder once more
each passing day / if each passing
day without faith is recoverable

*

empty the saltwater from the bowl
holding the rose quartz cluster
and slowly pour new saltwater over
the crystals / now the almost-full bowl

*

composed of turquoise the subconscious
beach / the tide cleans makeshift
changing rooms for sleeping chambers
/ yes the color is believed to fend off tigers

*

a he-runner victoriously in turquoise shorts
but does he know *turquoise* is derived
from Old French for *Turkish* / to want
to bathe with him / no / to want more

*

the twinks ignore a mint tea sipping gay
as they wait for to-go *macchiatos* /
he is twice their age / he is used to them /
he can never get used to this

*

an *i* surfaces as if from out of silhouette
/ out of desire / out of sleep / out of routine
/ out of doubt / out of the ground / out
he says *light light light light light light* into light

12 years of looking at nouns

1.   continents

from a northeast island
his all-consuming want

meanwhile in another

land a carefully composed
letter mentions reciprocation

and that it has stopped

2.   islands

he measures their distance

apart by the memories
of their arguments

yet his body remembers
pleasure and now this ferry

trip is the length of missing

3.   story

there once was a farm

a sick goat
a horny goat

several hens (minus one
after the fox inked the snow)

and a premonition of his ending

4.   fork

he thought he could eat

his way to a beginning
but this brought about

another ending and he
was forced to abandon

everything he knew

5.   hemispheres

as he sat on the stoop
the sun was nearer

but still far away

and the cold wind

he knew time was now
completely unfamiliar

6.   stadium

now he could see

who he was becoming
as it was happening

and the beautiful people
who were always there cheered

and he could forgive

7.   pen

darkness returns as darkness

nevertheless he's surprised
by the sounding ambulances

that aren't coming for him

as if a fence or a barn animal
looking for the fox

8.   ghost

this is another beginning
about ink

and there will be several

more to follow
before the ink

turns into someone else

9.   oars

more beautiful people

and a swan glides
elegantly across the pond

nevertheless he wants to jump
from a seafaring dinghy

and swim to another shore

10.   eggs

he's renewed again
by another

and another's language

a letter is written

and they will have
a dozen between them

11.   author

the distance between
words not being words

is narrowing

as is of course language

therefore it is time
to stop measuring

12.   obituaries

he is a bird now
on a doweled perch

on a doweled perch
he is a bird

among dried seed
the cage door opens

Hands
(a tribute)

That a *you* doesn't
exist, and one hundred
and two times over

faith is lost: a millipede
crawls under
a maybe-house: beforehand

the mind, my mind
is cut flowers: I lost
my body between

field and vases: and
the hornet against
the bathroom window

must not be killed.

Scattershot
(a tribute)

sound of elytra
against walls

against a ceiling
a beetle flies

into a lamp
the spiraling

until motionless
a dark spot on

a dark spot
in a glass dome

like now
a glass moon

and a shadow
under the trees

in a garden
yet countless

threads of light
on this shrub

a silvery wet
gray-green

almost the hue
of a mourning dove

almost the hue
of a cooing one

On Psalms

How without
surrounds me: these
not unfriendly

strangers: psalms

I seldom hear
and when I do
I don't sing

not because

I don't sing
or because
I don't believe

the words

but how I am
reminded: these
rituals

are not a part

of my vernacular
and I am
quieted

by gospel

Form
(a tribute)

Always one less breath.

Repeatedly I don't know
what will happen next.

Repeatedly I'm confused
by words, thousands
of words that all mean form.

*

Antonyms for form:
to exacerbate (or to distract)
to delineate (or to distract)

as is and so on and so forth.

*

The skeletal quality
of sideways
October light elicits
a rather-be-
forgotten memory.

*

A truth: my palms
flush against
the planes of my pelvis.

*

Without resistance

surrender
cannot be
surrender.

*

Infinity or rather
forever is relentless
and unrelenting.

I can't escape this

nomenclature: bone-
dry light defining

the unmade bed.

To accept needs
darkness which is not
the same as forever.

*

We need to be careful
what we ask for. *Are you*

certain that you're okay?

*

Empathy isn't considered
a proper noun in all instances.
I must remember

to capitalize "You."

*

My body is a trench.

To fall in.
To climb out of.

Morning light on my body.

Slope

This season
of my secret

anniversary

and now
anticipation

tilts then

disappears
into darkness

and among

this crystallization
an otherness

which keeps

Exordium

ending
becomes

last and *last*

becomes
salt

Acknowledgments

My warmest regards to the editors and staffs of the following
publications in which these poems first appeared, sometimes in
earlier versions.

About Place: "Prologue"
Apple Valley Review: "Plastic Speech"
Barrow Street: "Split Personality" and "On Psalms"
BLOOM: "A Bedrock"
Colorado Review: "It was not that long ago"
Contrary: "The Because"
Drunken Boat: "To Forest Hills Station"
Interim: "The Weight of Second Person"
Kenyon Review: "Tributary"
Konundrum Engine Literary Review: "Remarks on Nomenclature (a
tribute)"
Lodestar Quarterly: "Breathing Room" and "From Reticent's
Gazebo"
the luminary (U.K.)*:* "Neither sleeping nor waking"
MiPOesias: "Fertile Earth"
Poetry Midwest: "Hydrology: Aria"
Puerto del Sol: "Skin"
Queen City Review: "Silver Lake"
Southern Humanities Review: "Of Bones"
Spoon River Poetry Review: "Exordium"
three candles: "Hands (a tribute)"
Witness: "18 instances of overlooking descriptors"
Word For/Word: A Journal of New Writing "Faux Republique,"
"Itinerary (a tribute)," "Morning, Morning," and "Parse"

"Split Personality" appears in the anthology *Spaces Between Us*
(Third World Press, 2010)

I must provide heartfelt thanks to: Dwight and Diana McLellan for their love and generosity; Peter Covino for his prolonged enthusiasm for my poetry; Carrie Bennett for her tenacious guidance with not only this manuscript; Kate Faragher Houghton and Tanya Whiton for their unflinching support; my poetry family and especially Amaranth Borsuk, Anna Ross, Antonio Ochoa, Chad Arnold, Cheryl Clark Vermeulen, Connie Donovan, Derek Pollard, Gregory Lawless, Jessica Bozek, Judi Silverman, Megan Albert, Rob MacDonald, Rosann Kozlowski, Stephen Tapscott, and Talvikki Ansel; all of my teachers, yet especially Lissa Graham (Kennett High School), Ted Walker (New England College, U.K.), Mike Hayes (University of Central Lancashire), Betsy Sholl (University of Southern Maine), David Wojahn (Vermont College), Jack Myers (Vermont College), Jody Gladding (Vermont College), and Mark Cox (Vermont College); and to each of my students for teaching me something singularly remarkable.

Notes

Kevin McLellan earned BA's from the University of Southern Maine and the University of Central Lancashire, England, and an MFA in Writing from Vermont College. His poems have appeared in *American Letters & Commentary*, *Barrow Street*, *BLOOM*, *Colorado Review*, *Interim*, *Kenyon Review*, *Puerto del Sol*, *Southern Humanities Review*, *Western Humanities Review*, *Witness*, and many others. Kevin, originally from Conway, New Hampshire, currently lives and works in Cambridge, Massachusetts.

BARROW STREET POETRY